HEROES
OF THE US MILITARY

HEROES OF THE
U.S ARMY

By Barbara M. Linde

Gareth Stevens
Publishing

Please visit our website, www.garethstevens.com. For a free color catalog of all our high-quality books, call toll free 1-800-542-2595 or fax 1-877-542-2596.

Library of Congress Cataloging-in-Publication Data

Linde, Barbara M.
Heroes of the US Army / Barbara M. Linde.
    pages cm. — (Heroes of the US military)
Includes index.
ISBN 978-1-4339-7237-9 (pbk.)
ISBN 978-1-4339-7238-6 (6-pack)
ISBN 978-1-4339-7236-2 (library binding)
1. United States. Army—Juvenile literature. 2. Soldiers—United States—Juvenile literature. I. Title.
UA25.L6 2012
355.0092'273—dc23

2012000203

First Edition

Published in 2013 by
Gareth Stevens Publishing
111 East 14th Street, Suite 349
New York, NY 10003

Copyright © 2013 Gareth Stevens Publishing

Designer: Michael J. Flynn
Editor: Therese Shea

Photo credits: Cover, p. 1 DreamPictures/Blend Images/Getty Images; pp. 4–5 American School/
The Bridgeman Art Library/Getty Images; p. 6 Hulton Archive/Archive Photos/Getty Images;
p. 7 Fotosearch/Archive Photos/Getty Images; p. 8 rook76/Shutterstock.com; p. 9 Buyenlarge/
Archive Photos/Getty Images; courtesy of US Army: pp. 10 by Vets Incorporated, Wahpeton, ND, 12,
13, 15 by Ingrid Barrentine, 17, 20, 20–21 by Tina Miles, 780th MI Brigade, 22–23 by Staff Sgt. Lynette Hoke,
1st Brigade Combat Team, 34th Red Bull Infantry Division, 24 by Spc. David M. Sharp, 27, 29 by
Russell Sellers; p. 16 Andy Dean Photography/Shutterstock.com; p. 19 courtesy of NASA;
p. 28 courtesy of Crystalann Duarte.

Printed in the United States of America

CPSIA compliance information: Batch #CS12GS: For further information contact Gareth Stevens, New York, New York at 1-800-542-2595.

CONTENTS

Words in the glossary appear in **bold** type the first time they are used in the text.

A LONG AND PROUD HISTORY

The US Army is the oldest and largest branch of the United States military. Its main focus is land operations. The first US army, the Continental army, was formed in 1775 to help the American colonists fight for independence from England. George Washington was its commander. Under his skillful leadership, the colonies won the war.

The Mission

The army's duty, or mission, is to support national security and defense. Besides going to war against enemies, this mission includes helping friendly nations maintain peace. Army soldiers gather information about possible threats. They also rescue soldiers in danger, provide assistance during national **disasters**, and assist other military branches in their missions.

Since then, the United States has always had a standing army in times of war and peace. Brave army soldiers have fought both within and outside our borders to defend our freedom. Today, the army has over 488,000 active-duty soldiers, 189,000 **Army Reserve** soldiers, and more than 360,000 **National Guard** soldiers.

On the night of December 25, 1776, George Washington and his troops crossed the Delaware River into Trenton, New Jersey. This surprise attack resulted in an important victory for the Continental army.

THE FATHER OF THE MILITARY ACADEMY

Once the army began growing, its leaders needed a school to train soldiers. The United States Military Academy (USMA) was founded in 1802. Fortress West Point in New York was chosen as the location.

Sylvanus Thayer was an early student at West Point. During the War of 1812, Thayer's brilliant engineering ideas helped defend Norfolk, Virginia, from British capture. In 1817, he was asked to head the academy at West Point. His commitment to "duty, honor, country" became the school's official saying, or motto. Under Thayer's direction, West Point became an outstanding military academy and the first college of engineering in the United States.

Because of Sylvanus Thayer's focus on engineering, USMA graduates built most of the nation's first railway lines, bridges, harbors, and roads.

An Extraordinary West Point Graduate

Dwight D. Eisenhower graduated from West Point in 1915. A natural leader, he trained soldiers for **combat** in World War I and served in the Philippines. During World War II, he was the commanding general of army forces in Europe. Eisenhower served as president of the United States from 1953 to 1961. He helped end the **Korean War.**

"ANGEL OF THE BATTLEFIELD"

When the American Civil War began in 1861, Clara Barton rushed to help the wounded soldiers in Washington, DC. She later began taking food, clothing, and medical aid directly to the battlefields. Amid cannon fire and gunshots, she cared for soldiers in need.

The American Red Cross

Barton's war efforts led her to establish the American Red Cross in 1881. While the Red Cross is a private group led by volunteers, it works closely with the government. Today, its 1.3 million volunteers give relief to victims of war and disasters all over the world.

Clara Barton was honored with a US stamp in 1948.

UNITED STATES POSTAGE
FOUNDER OF THE
3¢
AMERICAN RED CROSS
CLARA BARTON

One doctor called Barton the "Angel of the Battlefield" after she risked her life to deliver supplies to the front at midnight. Barton also searched for missing soldiers and sent information to their families. While she was never in the army, she is a hero to the army. Her dedication and bravery made a difference to thousands of soldiers.

Clara Barton was president of the American Red Cross from 1881 to 1904. At this time, few women held positions of leadership.

COURAGE IN TWO WARS

Master Sergeant Woodrow W. Keeble earned four Purple Hearts and a Bronze Star during World War II. However, he received the army's highest award, the Medal of Honor, for his actions in the Korean War.

Master Sergeant Keeble was the first full-blooded Sioux Indian to receive the highest recognition for a soldier, the Medal of Honor.

In 1951, Keeble's unit fought to capture a hill that was protecting the enemy's supplies. Keeble found himself leading the unit after his commanding officers were killed. He recognized that three machine-gun posts had to be destroyed in order to move on safely. Though wounded by 83 **grenade** pieces, Keeble crawled up the hill alone with bullets flying all around him. Single-handedly, he took out all three posts. Only then did he order his men to advance.

Keeble at Guadalcanal

Guadalcanal is an island in the South Pacific, not far from Australia. Keeble fought in the Battle of Guadalcanal during World War II. After 6 months of fierce combat in 1942, forces including the United States defeated the Japanese. James Fenelon, a soldier who fought with Keeble at Guadalcanal, said, "The safest place to be was right next to Woody."

JUNGLE RESCUE

On May 2, 1968, Staff Sergeant Roy Benavidez jumped from a helicopter into the jungles of Vietnam in an effort to rescue wounded soldiers. Although he was severely wounded several times, Benavidez helped injured soldiers into a waiting helicopter. He was shot once more while retrieving secret papers that couldn't be left behind. At the same time, the helicopter pilot was killed, and the helicopter crashed.

Benavidez rescued soldiers from the helicopter and gave first aid while calling for help. When another helicopter arrived, he again loaded the wounded soldiers. He killed three enemy soldiers who tried to keep them from leaving. Finally, Benavidez managed to board the helicopter and escape.

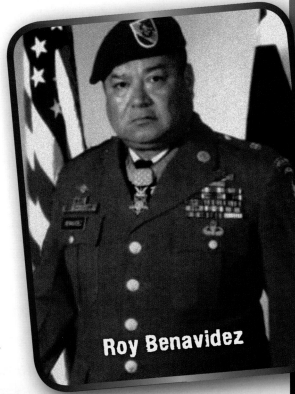

Roy Benavidez

Helicopters were a major part of the Vietnam War. More than 3,900 were used for combat and rescue.

The Medal of Honor

For his amazing actions in the **Vietnam War**, Roy Benavidez was awarded the Medal of Honor. The Medal of Honor is the highest military award and is given for extreme bravery in combat with the enemy. The first one was awarded in 1861. More than 3,400 members of the military have earned the medal since then.

The Army Rangers fight close-up battles with the enemy. They're trained to get the job done, no matter what, and no matter how many of their fellow soldiers fall.

On January 5, 2010, Staff Sergeant Austin McCall was in command of a Ranger unit in Afghanistan. He took the lead position searching a house. Inside, he came face-to-face with a bomber with two grenades. As they fought, the bomber threw one grenade and then fell to the floor with the other. McCall turned to warn his men just as the second grenade exploded. McCall's face was wounded by the explosion. Just then, enemy soldiers who had hidden in the house began to shoot.

The Army Rangers

The Army Rangers are a special operations force that is always ready for combat. Their high-risk missions include gathering information behind enemy lines and capturing enemy soldiers and territory. The Rangers promise they will "move further, faster and fight harder than any other soldier." They're called America's "no fail" force.

Of his heroics in January 2010, McCall said, "Any one of the Rangers would have done the same thing I did."

As the shooting began, the injured McCall kept fighting. He and his Rangers managed to secure the house.

McCall was treated for his wounds in Germany and spent less than a month back in the United States. Then he went back to his unit in Afghanistan.

Austin McCall received the Bronze Star with **Valor** and also the Purple Heart. He says he will continue fighting with his men. "I would have done it all over again, and I look forward to doing it all over again," McCall said. "That's the way we are. We are all Rangers—the best gunfighters in the world."

Bronze Star

Purple Heart

George Washington awards the honor now called the Purple Heart to Continental army soldiers in 1783.

Military Decorations

The Purple Heart is awarded to military members who are wounded in combat. First awarded in 1783 by George Washington, it was then called the "Badge of Military Merit." The Bronze Star Medal is awarded to a member of the army for heroism when fighting an armed enemy.

A SPACEWALKING SOLDIER

A few army soldiers, such as Colonel Doug Wheelock, have served in space! After graduating from West Point in 1983, Wheelock attended flight school and became an army pilot. In 1998, he began astronaut training. On his first spaceflight in 2007, Wheelock spent nearly 21 hours outside the space shuttle *Discovery* while repairing some damaged panels.

In 2010, Wheelock became the first active-duty army commander of the International Space Station (ISS). When part of the ISS's cooling system suddenly shut down, Wheeler performed three space walks to repair it. He received the American Red Cross 2010 Hero in Space Award.

The First Army Astronaut

Brigadier General Robert L. Stewart became the first army astronaut in 1979. He spent 289 hours in space on two space shuttle missions. His space walks totaled 12 hours. Stewart was one of two astronauts to test a jet pack that let astronauts move around outside the space shuttle without being tied to it.

Of his time in space, army astronaut Doug Wheelock said: "I know it's an opportunity of a lifetime, and I can serve our army and our country here as well."

THE CYBER BRIGADE

In the past, wars were fought on land, at sea, and in the air. Now, they're also fought in **cyberspace**. Enemies try to break into army computer systems. **Terrorists** use cell phones to operate bombs and e-mail to plan attacks. Some steal secret information and post it on the Internet. The army takes these security threats seriously.

The Army Emblem

The army emblem was first used in 1974. An emblem is an official sign. Each part of the army's emblem has a special meaning. In the middle of the emblem is a piece of Roman armor called a cuirass. It stands for strength. The weapons represent the firepower of the army.

The army's emblem is always shown in color and is used to represent the army.

On October 1, 2011, the 780th Military Intelligence **Brigade**, or Cyber Brigade, was established. Its mission is to fight the enemy through the Internet as well as defend our nation from cyber attacks. This special unit gathers information that could possibly stop future wars.

The Cyber Brigade conducts its first official run on December 2, 2011. Like other army units, these soldiers stay physically fit.

THE LAST TO LEAVE IRAQ

President Barack Obama greeted soldiers returning from Iraq on December 14, 2011: "As your commander in chief, and on behalf of a grateful nation, I am proud to finally say these two words—welcome home."

The 3rd Brigade Combat Team, "Greywolf," 1st Cavalry Division, crosses from Iraq into Kuwait on December 18, 2011.

First Sergeant Scott Dawson was among the last American troops to leave Iraq in December 2011. After four **deployments**, he was thrilled to greet his wife, Captain Jessica Dawson, and their children at Fort Hood, Texas. She is also an Iraq veteran. Since 2003, many families like the Dawsons had been spending months apart while their loved ones fought to establish a new government in Iraq.

The president praised the soldiers. He said, "You have shown why the US military is the finest fighting force in this great world."

The Last of Many

Army Specialist David Hickman was the last soldier killed in Iraq. On November 14, 2011, Hickman was riding in an armored truck that hit a roadside bomb. He died just 2 weeks before he was to go home. Nearly 4,500 American military were killed during the war in Iraq.

ARMY IN AFGHANISTAN

The US army has been fighting a war in Afghanistan since 2001. Many of today's military have fought in both Afghanistan and Iraq. Army Ranger Sergeant Leroy Petry served eight tours of duty in these countries.

On July 12, 2011, President Barack Obama awarded Leroy Petry the Medal of Honor at the White House in Washington, DC.

In 2011, Petry was awarded a Medal of Honor for his actions in Afghanistan. He threw a grenade back at the enemy after it landed near him and other Rangers. The grenade went off in flight, and Petry lost his hand. If he had not acted, he and his fellow soldiers might have been killed. Though grateful for the medal, Petry offered a simple reminder: "The greatest reward any service member can get is a simple 'thank you.' "

The Army Goes Rolling Along

The US Army song is called "The Army Goes Rolling Along." Its words start: "First to fight for the right/And to build the nation's might." The song remembers army battles and heroes. It reminds us that our nation's army will keep "rolling along" until its mission is complete.

In high school, Crystalann Duarte told her mother that she wanted to "join the military, travel the world, and fight the enemy." She lived that dream for 30 years during her time with the US Army.

Master Sergeant Duarte worked in the Transportation **Corps**. Her position was important to the success of army combat and noncombat missions. For a time, she loaded airplanes, trains, and ships with soldiers, weapons, and supplies. While working at a base in Germany in November 2001, she helped deploy the first wave of troops, gear, and vehicles that went to Iraq.

Transportation Corps

The Transportation Corps was established in 1942. Its motto is "Nothing happens until something moves." Members of this unit skillfully move large numbers of soldiers and gear from base to base within the United States and around the world. These soldiers make sure the military has the supplies it needs to complete each mission successfully.

Crystalann Duarte held the position of head stevedore with the Transportation Corps. A head stevedore oversees loading and unloading of army soldiers and supplies.

DUARTE

Crystalann Duarte retired from the army on July 22, 2009. As a member of the Peninsula Piecemakers Quilt Guild in Newport News, Virginia, Duarte now makes quilts for other heroic warriors.

In Bosnia, Duarte organized gear needed to remove land mines. Terrorists in Honduras shot at her while she built a road. She also transported materials to fight oil fires in Saudi Arabia. Back in the United States, Duarte worked for the US Department of Defense. There, she made sure that the bodies of soldiers who died in combat were safely returned and that their families were properly notified.

Crystalann Duarte received the Bronze Star NATO Medal in Saudi Arabia and the Expeditionary Medal in Bosnia. "I loved what I did, and I would do it again," she says. Duarte's story reminds us that not all army heroes are in the news.

Quilts of Valor

Duarte spent some time at the Fort Belvoir Hospital. There, she was given a Quilt of Valor. This organization of quilters all over the country has made more than 37,000 quilts for men and women who have returned from war. Families of those who sacrifice their lives also receive Quilts of Valor.

More than 20 soldiers received quilts from the Quilts of Valor organization at Lyster Army Health Clinic in Alabama on May 26, 2011.

GLOSSARY

Army Reserve: part-time soldiers who are called to duty when needed

brigade: a military unit consisting of two or more combat units called battalions

combat: armed fighting between opposing forces. Also, to fight against someone or something.

corps: a group of soldiers trained for special service

cyberspace: the online world of computer networks. The Internet.

deployment: the act of positioning troops and resources so they are ready for action

disaster: an event that causes much suffering and loss

grenade: a small bomb thrown by hand or using a launcher

Korean War: a conflict between North and South Korea that began in 1950 and ended in 1953 in which the United States joined with South Korea

National Guard: a state military force under the command of the governor

terrorist: someone who uses violence and fear to challenge an authority

valor: bravery

Vietnam War: a conflict starting in 1955 and ending in 1975 between South Vietnam and North Vietnam in which the United States joined with South Vietnam

FOR MORE INFORMATION

Books

Hamilton, John. *United States Army*. Edina, MN: ABDO Publishing, 2012.

Llanas, Sheila Griffen. *Women of the U.S. Army: Pushing Limits*. Mankato, MN: Capstone Press, 2011.

Simons, Lisa M. Bolt. *Soldiers of the U.S. Army*. Mankato, MN: Capstone Press, 2009.

Websites

American Battle Monuments Commission
www.abmc.gov
Take virtual tours of some historic army battle sites.

The Army Historical Foundation
www.armyhistory.org
Use this site to learn more about army history.

The Official Homepage of the United States Army
www.army.mil
Learn about the latest army news.

INDEX